DOVER · THRIFT · EDITIONS

Wit and Wisdom from Poor Richard's Almanack

BENJAMIN FRANKLIN

DOVER PUBLICATIONS, INC.
Mineola, New York

DOVER THRIFT EDITIONS

GENERAL EDITOR: PAUL NEGRI
EDITOR OF THIS VOLUME: KATHY CASEY

Copyright

Copyright © 1999 by Dover Publications, Inc.
All rights reserved under Pan American and International Copyright Conventions.

Published in Canada by General Publishing Company, Ltd., 30 Lesmill Road, Don Mills, Toronto, Ontario.

Bibliographical Note

Wit and Wisdom from Poor Richard's Almanack is a new selection of quotations from various editions of *Poor Richard's Almanack*, originally published by Benjamin Franklin in Philadelphia for the years 1733–1758.

Library of Congress Cataloging-in-Publication Data

Franklin, Benjamin, 1706–1790.
    [Poor Richard. Selections]
    Wit and wisdom from Poor Richard's almanack / Benjamin Franklin.
        p.   cm. — (Dover thrift editions)
    ISBN 0-486-40891-4
    1. Maxims, American.   I. Title.   II. Series.
PS749.A6   1999
818'.102—dc21   99-30702
                                                                               CIP

Manufactured in the United States of America
Dover Publications, Inc., 31 East 2nd Street, Mineola, N.Y. 11501

Note

BENJAMIN FRANKLIN (1706–1790), a man of many talents and prodigious accomplishments, was well known and admired in Great Britain's American colonies during the decades prior to the establishment of the United States of America, in which he played a major role. Active in promoting police and fire services, a free public library, public hospital services, and higher education, he was already prominent in Philadelphia as a businessman, inventor, and civic leader when he served as a delegate to the Second Continental Congress and helped draft the Declaration of Independence in 1776. He then became a very popular diplomatic representative to France, successfully seeking military and financial aid for the colonists' war to gain independence.

At the age of 12 (having ended his formal education two years earlier) Franklin was apprenticed to an older brother, a printer. He later worked at that trade in Philadelphia and London. When he was established in Philadelphia, he began publishing a newspaper, the *Pennsylvania Gazette*, and in 1732 produced the first edition of *Poor Richard's Almanack*, using the pen name Richard Saunders and inventing a persona for the "author" and his equally imaginary wife, Bridget. Along with the usual astronomical and other data, information for travelers, and some factual articles, each almanac included dozens of proverbs, both witty and solemn aphorisms, advice on health and wealth, strictures on virtuous living, and humorous verses.

For a quarter of a century (1733–1758), *Poor Richard's Almanack* was widely read, frequently quoted, and vastly enjoyed. As Franklin acknowledged, the pithy sayings presented in *Poor Richard's Almanack* reflected "the wisdom of many ages and nations" and were not all original to him. However, the beliefs, wit, and wisdom of this genial, immensely energetic, creative man who lived life fully are evident throughout this selection from the writings of "Poor Richard."

Contents

Aging and Youth

An old young man will be a young old man.

*

Youth is pert and positive, Age modest and doubting: So Ears of Corn when young and light, stand bold upright, but hang their Heads when weighty, full, and ripe.

*

All would live long, but none would be old.

*

At 20 years of age the Will reigns; at 30 the Wit; at 40 the Judgment.

Anger, Revenge, Forgiveness

If *Passion* drives, Let *Reason* hold the Reins.

*

Take heed of the Vinegar of sweet Wine, and the Anger of Good-nature.

Are you angry that others disappoint you? remember you cannot depend upon yourself.

*

A Man in a Passion rides a mad Horse.

*

Anger warms the Invention, but overheats the Oven.

*

It is better to take many injuries, than to give one.

*

Neglect kills Injuries, Revenge increases them.

*

If you would be reveng'd of your enemy, govern yourself.

*

Anger is never without a Reason, but seldom with a good One.

*

He is a Governor that governs his Passions,
and he a Servant that serves them.

Doing an Injury puts you below your Enemy;
Revenging one makes you but even with him;
Forgiving it sets you above him.

*

The end of Passion is the beginning of Repentance.

*

Anger and Folly walk check by-jole;
Repentance treads on both their Heels.

*

Take this remark from *Richard* poor and lame,
Whate'er's begun in anger ends in shame.

CLEVERNESS AND CRAFTINESS

Cunning proceeds from Want of Capacity.

*

Many Foxes grow grey, but few grow good.

*

Craft must be at charge for clothes,
but *Truth* can go naked.

You may be too cunning for One, but not for All.

CONTENTMENT
AND DISCONTENTMENT

Content makes poor men rich; Discontent makes rich Men poor.

*

The discontented Man finds no easy Chair.

*

When you taste Honey, remember Gall.

*

Better is a little with content than much with contention.

*

He that's content, hath enough;
He that complains, hath too much.

*

Wealth and Content are not always Bed-fellows.

A wise Man will desire no more, than what he may get justly, use soberly, distribute chearfully, and leave contentedly.

*

The Poor have little, Beggars none;
the Rich too much, enough not one.

*

Content is the Philosopher's Stone, that turns all it touches into Gold.

*

Discontented Minds, and Fevers of the Body
are not to be cured by changing Beds or Businesses.

*

Content and Riches seldom meet together,
Riches take thou, contentment I had rather.

*

We are not so sensible of the greatest Health as of the least Sickness.

*

Who is rich? He that rejoices in his portion.

If Man could have Half his Wishes, he would double his Troubles.

*

CONTENTMENT! Parent of Delight,
So much a Stranger to our Sight,
Say, Goddess, in what happy Place
Mortals behold thy blooming Face;
Thy gracious Auspices impart,
And for thy Temple chuse my Heart.
They whom thou deignest to inspire,
Thy Science learn, to bound Desire;
By happy Alchymy of Mind
They turn to Pleasure all they find.
Unmov'd when the rude Tempest blows,
Without an Opiate they repose;
And, cover'd by your Shield, defy
The whizzing Shafts that round them fly;
Nor, meddling with the Gods Affairs,
Concern themselves with distant Cares;
But place their Bliss in mental Rest,
And feast upon the Good possest.

DECEIT AND TRUST

There's none deceived, but he that trusts.

*

In the Affairs of this World Men are saved, not by Faith, but by the Want of it.

None are deceived but they that confide.

＊

He that sells upon trust, loses many friends, and always wants money.

DILIGENCE AND SLOTH

The sleeping Fox catches no poultry.

＊

Diligence overcomes Difficulties, Sloth makes them.

＊

Employ thy time well, if thou meanest to gain leisure.

＊

Plough deep while Sluggards sleep; and you shall have Corn to sell and to keep.

＊

Laziness travels so slowly that Poverty soon overtakes him.

＊

Be always ashamed to catch thyself idle.

Idleness is the Dead Sea, that swallows all Virtues.

*

No man e'er was glorious, who was not laborious.

*

The idle Man is the Devil's Hireling; whose Livery is Rags, whose Diet and Wages are Famine and Diseases.

*

Trouble springs from *Idleness; Toil* from *Ease.*

*

God helps them that help themselves.

*

Diligence is the mother of good luck.

EATING AND DRINKING

Dine with little, sup with less: Do better still: sleep supperless.

*

Tim moderate fare and abstinence much prizes,
In publick, but in private gormandizes.

A full Belly is the Mother of all Evil.

*

Eat to live; live not to eat.

*

A fat kitchin, a lean Will.

*

Sleep without Supping, and you'll rise without owing for it.

*

If it were not for the Belly, the Back might wear Gold.

*

When the Wine enters, out goes the Truth.

*

To lengthen thy Life, lessen thy Meals.

*

Hot things, sharp things, sweet things, cold things
All rot the teeth, and make them look like old things.

*

Eat few suppers, and you'll need few Medicines.

He that drinks fast, pays slow.

*

Nothing more like a Fool, than a drunken Man.

*

Cheese and salt meat should be sparingly eat.

*

Many Dishes, many Diseases.

*

Never spare the Parson's wine, nor the Baker's pudding.

*

He that would travel much, should eat little.

*

Drink Water, Put the Money in your Pocket, and leave the *Dry-bellyach* in the *Punchbowl.*

*

A full Belly makes a dull Brain.

*

He that never eats too much, will never be lazy.

Drink does not drown Care, but waters it, and makes it grow faster.

*

Hunger never saw bad bread.

*

What one relishes, nourishes.

FOLLY

Experience keeps a dear school, yet Fools will learn in no other.

*

He that spills the Rum loses that only; He that drinks it, often loses both that and himself.

*

To-morrow I'll reform, the fool does say;
To-day itself's too late;—the *wise* did yesterday.

*

If evils come not, then our fears are vain;
And if they do, fear but augments the pain.

*

They who have nothing to be troubled at, will be troubled at nothing.

A learned Blockhead is a greater Blockhead than an ignorant one.

*

He that resolves to mend hereafter, resolves not to mend now.

*

Fools need Advice most, but wise Men only are the better for it.

*

He's a Fool that makes his Doctor his Heir.

*

The learned Fool writes his Nonsense in better Language than the unlearned; but still 'tis Nonsense.

*

Is there anything men take more pains about than to make themselves unhappy?

*

To whom thy secret thou dost tell, to him thy freedom thou dost sell.

The first Degree of Folly, is to conceit one's self wise; the second to profess it; the third to despise Counsel.

*

He that pursues two hares at once, does not catch one and lets t'other go.

*

Silence is not always a Sign of Wisdom, but Babbling is ever a Folly.

*

A little Neglect may breed great Mischief: For want of a Nail the Shoe is lost; for want of a Shoe the Horse is lost; for want of a Horse the Rider is lost.

*

There are no fools so troublesome as those that have wit.

*

It is Ill-Manners to silence a Fool, and Cruelty to let him go on.

*

Sloth and silence are a fool's virtues.

FRIENDSHIP

No better relation than a prudent and faithful friend.

*

Be slow in chusing a Friend, slower in changing.

*

A Brother may not be a Friend, but a Friend will always be a Brother.

*

Friendship cannot live with Ceremony, nor without Civility.

*

There are three faithful friends—an old wife, an old dog, and ready money.

*

Thou canst not joke an Enemy into a Friend; but thou may'st a Friend into an Enemy.

*

Friendship increases by visiting Friends, but by visiting seldom.

'Tis great Confidence in a Friend to tell him your Faults, greater to tell him his.

*

A false Friend and a Shadow attend only while the Sun shines.

*

When befriended, remember it:
When you befriend, forget it.

*

When a Friend deals with a Friend, let the bargain be clear and well penn'd, that they may continue Friends to the End.

*

The same man cannot be both Friend and Flatterer.

*

A true Friend is the best Possession.

GOOD CONSCIENCE

A quiet Conscience sleeps in Thunder,
but Rest and Guilt live far asunder.

Keep Conscience clear,
then never fear.

*

If thou injurest Conscience, it will have its Revenge
on thee.

*

E're you remark another's Sin,
Bid your own Conscience look within.

*

The nearest way to come at glory, is to do that for
conscience which we do for glory.

GREED, MISERLINESS

Ambition often spends foolishly what *Avarice* had
wickedly collected.

*

Wish a miser a long life, and you wish him no good.

*

If your Riches are yours, why don't you take them
with you to t'other World?

Poverty wants some things, Luxury many things, Avarice all things.

*

He does not possess Wealth, it possesses him.

*

Avarice and Happiness never saw each other, how then shou'd they become acquainted.

*

Tell a miser he's rich, and a woman she's old, you'll get no money of one, nor kindness of t'other.

HAPPINESS

Enjoy the present hour, be mindful of the past;
And neither fear nor wish the approaches of the last.

*

Virtue & Happiness are Mother & Daughter.

*

Who pleasure gives,
Shall joy receive.

Love, and be *loved.*

HONESTY AND DISHONESTY

Half the Truth is often a great Lie.

*

The honest Man takes Pains, and then enjoys
Pleasures; the Knave takes Pleasure, and then suf-
fers Pains.

*

Avoid dishonest Gain: No price
Can recompence the Pangs of Vice.

*

'Tis hard (but glorious) to be poor and honest: An
empty Sack can hardly stand upright; but if it does,
'tis a stout one!

*

Men take more pains to mask than mend.
Bad Gains are truly Losses.

*

What pains our Justice takes his faults to hide,
With half that pains sure he might cure 'em quite.

An honest Man will receive neither *Money* nor *Praise*, that is not his Due.

MEN, WOMEN, AND MARRIAGE

One good Husband is worth two good Wives; for the scarcer things are, the more they're valued.

*

He that goes far to marry, will either deceive or be deceived.

*

Let thy maid-servant be faithful, strong, and homely.

*

He that has not got a Wife, is not yet a compleat Man.

*

Marry above thy match, and thou 'lt get a master.

*

You can bear your own Faults, and why not a Fault in your Wife.

Grief often treads upon the heels of pleasure,
Marry'd in haste, we oft repent at leisure;
Some by experience find these words misplaced,
Marry'd at leisure, they repent in haste.
Wedlock, as old men note, hath likened been
Unto a public crowd or common rout;
Where those that are without would fain get in,
And those that are within, would fain get out.

*

A good wife lost, is God's gift lost.

*

He that takes a wife takes Care.

*

A house without woman and firelight, is like a body
without soul or sprite.

*

Where there's Marriage without Love, there will be
Love without Marriage.

*

Keep your eyes wide open before marriage, half
shut afterwards.

*

The good or ill hap of a good or ill life,
is the good or ill choice of a good or ill wife.

The proof of gold is fire, the proof of woman, gold; the proof of man, a woman.

*

Ne'er take a wife till thou hast a house (& a fire) to put her in.

*

If *Jack's* in love, he's no judge of *Jill's* beauty.

*

A good Wife & Health, is a Man's best Wealth.

*

You cannot pluck roses without fear of thorns, Nor enjoy a fair wife without danger of horns.

MONEY AND FRUGALITY

He that speaks ill of the Mare, will buy her.

*

He that can travel well afoot, keeps a good horse.

*

Keep thy shop, and thy shop will keep thee.

If you'd know the Value of Money, go and borrow some.

*

Necessity never made a good bargain.

*

A penny saved is two pence clear. A pin a-day is a groat a-year. Save and have.

*

Pay what you owe, and what you're worth you'll know.

*

'Tis against some Mens Principle to pay Interest, and seems against others Interest to pay the Principal.

*

He that is rich need not live sparingly, and he that can live sparingly need not be rich.

*

Great spenders are bad lenders.

*

If you know how to spend less than you get, you have the philosopher's stone.

Bargaining has neither friends nor relations.

*

Spare and have is better than *spend and crave*.

*

Beware of little Expenses: a small Leak will sink a great Ship.

*

He that is of Opinion Money will do every Thing may well be suspected of doing every Thing for Money.

*

Many have been ruin'd by buying good penny-worths.

*

Ask and have, is sometimes dear buying.

*

Idleness is the greatest Prodigality.

*

Buy what thou hast no need of, and e'er long thou shalt sell thy necessaries.

*

Creditors have better memories than debtors.

Rather go to bed supperless than run in debt for a breakfast.

*

For Age and Want save while you may; No morning Sun lasts a whole Day.

*

All things are cheap to the saving, dear to the wasteful.

*

The Creditors are a superstitious sect, great observers of set days and times.

*

Money & Man a mutual Friendship show:
Man makes *false* Money, Money makes Man so.

*

Every little makes a mickle.

*

The use of money is all the advantage there is in having money.

*

For 6£ a year you may have use of 100£, if you are a man of known prudence and honesty.

He that spends a groat a-day idly, spends idly above 6£ a year, which is the price of using 100£.

*

He that wastes idly a groat's worth of his time per day one day with another, wastes the privilege of using 100£ each day.

*

He that idly loses 5s. worth of time, loses 5s., and might as prudently throw 5s. into the river. He that loses 5s. not only loses that sum, but all the other advantages that might be made by turning it in dealing, which by the time a young man becomes old, amounts to a comfortable bag of money.

PRIDE, VANITY

He that falls in love with himself will have no rivals.

*

Pride dines upon Vanity, sups on Contempt.

*

A flatterer never seems absurd: The flatter'd always takes his word.

*

Pride gets into the Coach, and *Shame* mounts behind.

Great Pride and Meanness sure are near ally'd;
Or thin Partitions do their Bounds divide.

*

Declaiming against Pride, is not always a Sign of
Humility.

*

Vanity backbites more than *Malice*.

*

Fond Pride of Dress is sure an empty Curse;
E're *Fancy* you consult, consult your Purse.

*

As Pride increases, Fortune declines.

*

Vain-glory flowereth, but beareth no Fruit.

*

Pride is as loud a Beggar as *Want*,
and a great deal more saucy.

*

The Proud hate Pride—in others.

*

As sore places meet most rubs, proud folks meet
most affronts.

To be proud of Knowledge, is to be blind with Light.

*

Pride breakfasted with *Plenty*, dined with *Poverty*, supped with *Infamy*.

PROFESSIONS AND OCCUPATIONS

A country man between two lawyers, is like a fish between two cats.

*

A good lawyer, a bad neighbour.

*

Sound, & sound Doctrine, may pass through a Ram's Horn, and a Preacher, without straightening the one, or amending the other.

*

Beware of the young doctor and the old barber.

*

He's the best physician that knows the worthlessness of the most medicines.

*

There's more old drunkards, than old doctors.

God heals, and the Doctor takes the fees.

*

He that has a Trade has an Office of Profit and Honour.

PROSPERITY AND SUCCESS

Prosperity discovers Vice, Adversity, Virtue.

*

Many a Man would have been worse, if his Estate had been better.

*

He that would catch Fish, must venture his Bait.

*

A Change of *Fortune* hurts a wise Man no more than a Change of the *Moon*.

*

Wealth is not his that has it, but his that enjoys it.

*

Success has ruin'd many a Man.

Industry, Perseverance, & Frugality, make Fortune yield.

*

No gains without pains.

*

He that pays for Work before it's done,
has but a pennyworth for twopence.

*

He that can have patience can have what he will.

*

In success, be moderate.

*

When *Prosperity* was well mounted, she let go the Bridle, and soon came tumbling out of the Saddle.

*

He who multiplies Riches multiplies Cares.

PRUDENCE, GOOD SENSE

Make haste slowly.

If your head is wax, don't walk in the Sun.

*

Keep your mouth wet, feet dry.

*

Be not sick too late, nor well too soon.

*

The way to be safe, is never to be secure.

*

Don't misinform your Doctor nor your Lawyer.

*

Three may keep a secret, if two of them are dead.

*

An egg to-day is better than a hen to-morrow.

*

Take counsel in wine, but resolve afterwards in water.

*

Don't go to the doctor with every distemper, nor to the lawyer with every quarrel, nor to the pot for every thirst.

A Slip of the Foot you may soon recover, but a slip of the Tongue you may never get over.

*

Love your Neighbor; yet don't pull down your Hedge.

*

He that waits upon fortune, is never sure of a dinner.

*

Learn of the skilful; He that teaches himself, hath a fool for his master.

*

Hold your Council before Dinner; the full Belly hates Thinking as well as Acting.

*

Haste makes waste.

*

Don't throw Stones at your Neighbours', if your own Windows are Glass.

*

Forewarn'd, forearm'd.

'Tis easier to suppress the first Desire, than to satisfy all that follow it.

*

If you'd have a servant that you like, serve yourself.

*

Look before, or you'll find yourself behind.

*

Great Estates may venture more; Little Boats must keep near Shore.

*

'Tis easier to prevent bad habits than to break them.

*

Blessed is he that expects nothing, for he shall never be disappointed.

*

Good Sense is a Thing all need, few have, and none think they want.

*

The favour of the Great is no inheritance.

*

Ceremony is not Civility; nor Civility Ceremony.

There's small Revenge in Words, but Words may be greatly revenged.

*

Let thy Discontents be Secrets.

*

Dally not with other Folks Women or Money.

*

There's a time to wink as well as to see.

*

He that would live in peace & at ease,
Must not speak all he knows, nor judge all he sees.

*

Keep flax from fire, youth from gaming.

PUBLIC AFFAIRS

Happy that Nation,—fortunate that age, whose history is not diverting.

*

When there's no Law, there's no Bread.

Singularity in the right, hath ruined many; happy those who are convinced of the general Opinion.

*

In Rivers and bad Governments, the lightest things swim at top.

*

Laws *too gentle* are seldom *obeyed*;
too severe, seldom *executed*.

*

The magistrate should obey the laws, the people should obey the magistrate.

*

To serve the Publick faithfully, and at the same time please it entirely, is impracticable.

*

You may give a Man an Office, but you cannot give him Discretion.

*

The church, the state, and the poor, are 3 daughters which we should maintain, but not portion off.

*

The first Mistake in public Business, is the going into it.

Pardoning the Bad, is injuring the Good.

*

Without justice, courage is weak.

*

Where there is Hunger, Law is not regarded; and where Law is not regarded, there will be Hunger.

*

The Good-will of the Governed will be starv'd, if not fed by the good Deeds of the Governors.

*

He that cannot obey, cannot command.

*

Laws like to *Cobwebs* catch small Flies,
Great ones break thro' before your eyes.

RELIGION

Many have quarrel'd about Religion, that never practised it.

*

You will be careful, if you are wise, how you touch men's Religion, or Credit, or Eyes.

The Way to see by *Faith* is to shut the Eye of *Reason:* The Morning Daylight appears plainer when you put out your Candle.

*

Fear not death; for the sooner we die, the longer shall we be immortal.

*

Prayers and Provender hinder no Journey.

*

The painful Preacher, like a candle bright,
Consumes himself in giving others Light.

*

Different sects like different clocks, may be all near the matter, 'tho they don't quite agree.

*

'Tis not a Holiday that's not kept holy.

*

What is Serving God? 'Tis doing Good to Man.

*

Christianity commands us to pass by Injuries;
Policy, to let them pass by us.

Talking against Religion is unchaining a Tyger; the Beast let loose may worry his Deliverer.

*

Sin is not hurtful because it is forbidden but it is forbidden because it is hurtful.

*

Think of three Things — whence you came, where you are going, and to Whom you must account.

*

Serving God is Doing Good to Man, but Praying is thought an easier Service, and therefore more generally chosen.

SELF-AWARENESS

Observe all men; thyself most.

*

Search others for their virtues, thy self for thy vices.

*

The Sting of a Reproach, is the Truth of it.

Wink at small faults—remember thou hast great ones.

*

A man of knowledge like a rich soil, feeds
If not a world of corn, a world of weeds.

*

Many a Man thinks he is buying Pleasure, when he is really selling himself a Slave to it.

*

Neglect mending a small Fault, and 'twill soon be a great One.

*

Love your Enemies, for they tell you your Faults.

*

Who has deceiv'd thee so oft as thy self?

SELF-DEVELOPMENT

Hide not your Talents, they for Use were made:
What's a Sun-Dial in the Shade?

*

Tho' Modesty is a Virtue, Bashfulness is a Vice.

Genius without Education is like Silver in the Mine.

*

Early to bed and early to rise, makes a man healthy, wealthy, and wise.

*

Reading makes a full man—Meditation a profound man—Discourse a clear man.

*

He that can bear a Reproof, and mend by it, if he is not wise, is in a fair way of being so.

*

Being ignorant is not so much a Shame, as being unwilling to learn.

*

It is not Leisure that is not used.

*

If thou hast wit & learning, add to it Wisdom and Modesty.

*

Be at War with your Vices, at Peace with your Neighbours, and let every New-Year find you a better Man.

Read much; the Mind, which never can be still,
If not intent on Good, is prone to Ill.
And where bright Thoughts, or Reas'nings just you
    find,
Repose them careful in your inmost Mind.

SOCIAL RELATIONS

Ill customs and bad advice are seldom forgotten.

*

Eat to please thyself, but dress to please others.

*

Great Good-nature, without Prudence, is a great
Misfortune.

*

He that drinks his Cyder alone, let him catch his
Horse alone.

*

An open foe may prove a curse; but a pretended
friend is worse.

*

Quarrels never could last long, if on one side only
lay the wrong.

Tart Words make no Friends; a spoonful of honey will catch more flies than a Gallon of Vinegar.

*

Neither trust, nor contend, nor lay wagers, nor lend; and you'll have peace to your Lives' end.

*

When you speak to a man, look on his eyes; when he speaks to thee, look on his mouth.

*

There is much difference between imitating a good man, and counterfeiting him.

*

If you'd lose a troublesome Visitor, lend him money.

*

Fish and visitors stink after three days.

*

Promises may get thee friends, but non-performance will turn them into enemies.

*

Praise little, dispraise less.

Those who are fear'd, are hated.

*

A man without ceremony has need of great merit in its place.

*

He that lieth down with dogs, shall rise up with fleas.

*

Men and melons are hard to know.

*

Beware of meat twice boil'd, and an old foe reconcil'd.

*

He that won't be counsell'd, can't be help'd.

*

Act uprightly and despise Calumny; Dirt may stick to a Mud Wall, but not to polish'd Marble.

*

A quarrelsome Man has no good Neighbors.

We must give Advice, but we cannot give Conduct.

*

He that scatters thorns, let him not go barefoot.

*

The rotten apple spoils his companion.

*

There is no little enemy.

*

Suspicion may be no fault, but showing it may be a great one.

*

Be civil to all; sociable to many; familiar with few; Friend to one; Enemy to none.

*

Beware of him that is slow to anger: He is angry for something, and will not be pleased for nothing.

*

Visits should be short, like a winters day,
Lest you're too troublesom hasten away.

TALKING AND SILENCE

He that speaks much, is much mistaken.

*

If you have no Honey in your Pot, have some in your Mouth.

*

The Tongue offends, and the Ears get the cuffing.

*

When Man and Woman die, as Poets sung,
His Heart's the last part moves, her last, the tongue.

*

You may talk too much on the best of subjects.

*

Proclaim not all thou knowest, all thou owest, all thou hast, nor all thou canst.

*

As we must account for every idle word, so we must for every idle silence.

*

A soft Tongue may strike hard.

Mary's mouth costs her nothing,
for she never opens it but at others expence.

*

In a discreet man's mouth, a publick thing is private.

*

Half Wits talk much but say little.

*

Teach your child to hold his tongue,
he'll learn fast enough to speak.

*

Many a Man's own Tongue gives Evidence against
his Understanding.

TIME

One *To-day* is worth two *To-morrows.*

*

Lost Time is never found again.

*

You may delay, but *Time* will not.

If you have time don't wait for time.

*

Employ thy time well, if thou meanest to gain leisure.

*

He that riseth late, must trot all day, and shall scarce overtake his business at night.

*

Dost thou love Life? Then do not squander Time; for that's the Stuff Life is made of.

*

Time is an herb that cures all Diseases.

*

Have you somewhat to do to-morrow, do it to-day.

*

Time enough, always proves *little enough*.

*

Prodigality of *Time*, produces Poverty of Mind as well as of Estate.

Since thou art not sure of a minute, throw not away an hour.

VICE

Monkeys, warm with envious spite, their most obliging friends will bite.

*

Tricks and treachery are the practice of fools that have not wit enough to be honest.

*

What maintains one Vice would bring up two children.

*

People who are wrapped up in themselves make small packages.

*

Each year one vicious habit rooted out,
In time might make the worst Man good throughout.

*

Let thy vices die before thee.

The second Vice is Lying; the first is running in Debt.

*

Vice knows she's ugly, so puts on her Mask.

*

Virtue may not always make a Face handsome, but *Vice* will certainly make it ugly.

VIRTUE

Well done is better than well said.

*

Have you somewhat to do to-morrow, do it today.

*

How few there are who have courage enough to own their own Faults, or resolution enough to mend them!

*

Nor eye in a letter, nor hand in a purse, nor ear in the secret of another.

*

What you would seem to be, be really.

He is ill cloth'd, who is bare of Virtue.

*

Who is strong? He that can conquer his bad Habits.

*

Be not niggardly of what costs thee nothing, as courtesy, counsel, and countenance.

*

Hear no ill of a friend, nor speak any of an enemy.

*

Seek Virtue, and, of that possest,
To Providence, resign the rest.

*

It is wise not to seek a Secret, and Honest not to reveal it.

*

An innocent plowman is more worthy than a vicious prince.

*

Do not do that which you would not have known.

*

A good Example is the best Sermon.

Virtue and a Trade, are a Child's best Portion.

*

Humility makes great men twice honourable.

*

Would you live with ease, do what you ought, and not what you please.

The Thirteen Virtues:

1. Temperance: Eat not to dullness. Drink not to elevation.

*

2. Silence: Speak not but what may benefit others or yourself. Avoid trifling conversation.

*

3. Order: Let all your things have their places. Let each part of your business have its time.

*

4. Resolution: Resolve to perform what you ought. Perform without fail what you resolve.

5. Frugality: Make no expense but to do good to others or yourself; i.e., waste nothing.

*

6. Industry: Lose no time. Be always employed in something useful. Cut off all unnecessary actions.

*

7. Sincerity: Use no hurtful deceit. Think innocently and justly; if you speak, speak accordingly.

*

8. Justice: Wrong none by doing injuries or omitting the benefits that are your duty.

*

9. Moderation: Avoid extremes. Forbear resenting injuries so much as you think they deserve.

*

10. Cleanliness: Tolerate no uncleanliness in body, clothes, or habitation.

*

11. Tranquility: Be not disturbed at trifles or at accidents common or unavoidable.

12. Chastity: Rarely use venery but for health or off-
spring—never to dullness, weakness, or the injury of
your own or another's peace or reputation.

*

13. Humility: Imitate Jesus and Socrates.

*

Let no pleasure tempt thee, no profit allure thee, no
ambition corrupt thee, no example sway thee, no
persuasion move thee, to do any thing which thou
knowest to be evil; so shalt thou always live
jollily . . .

DIVERSE CONSIDERATIONS

After 3 days men grow weary, of a wench, a guest, &
weather rainy.

*

Relationship without friendship, friendship without
power, power without will, will without effect, effect
without profit, & profit without vertue, are not
worth a farto.

*

Neither a Fortress nor a Maidenhead will hold out
long after they begin to parley.

Bad Commentators spoil the best of books.

*

Paintings and Fightings are best seen at a distance.

*

There's many witty men whose brains can't fill their bellies.

*

Of learned fools I have seen ten times ten,
Of unlearned wise men I have seen a hundred.

*

Great Modesty often hides great Merit.

*

There have been as great Souls unknown to fame as any of the most famous.

*

None preaches better than the ant, and she says nothing.

*

Neither trust, nor contend, nor lay wagers, nor lend;
And you'll have peace to your Lives end.

The absent are never without fault, nor the present without excuse.

*

Mankind are very odd Creatures: One Half censure what they practise, the other half practise what they censure; the rest always say and do as they ought.

*

Some are weatherwise, some are otherwise.

*

He that would have a short Lent,
Let him borrow Money to be repaid at Easter.

*

Beauty & folly are old companions.

*

To err is human, to repent divine, to persist devilish.

*

Don't judge of Mens Wealth or Piety,
by their *Sunday* Appearances.

*

If you desire many things, many things will seem but a few.

When you're an Anvil, hold you still;
When you're a Hammer, strike your Fill.

*

He that can take rest is greater than he that can take cities.

*

Old Boys have their Playthings as well as young Ones; the Difference is only in the Price.

*

Love, Cough, & a Smoke, can't well be hid.

*

Wouldst thou confound thine Enemy, be good thy self.

*

There are no ugly Loves, nor handsome Prisons.

*

He that lives upon Hope will die fasting.

*

Write with the learned, pronounce with the vulgar.

I never saw an oft-transplanted tree,
Nor yet an oft-removed family,
That throve so well as those that settled be.

*

Sell not Virtue to purchase wealth, nor Liberty to purchase power.

*

Wish not so much to live long as to live well.

*

To bear other people's afflictions, every one has courage and enough to spare.

*

When the Well's dry, we know the Worth of Water.

*

A Ship under sail and a big-bellied Woman, are the handsomest two things that can be seen common.

*

The Muses love the Morning.

*

Glass, China, and Reputation, are easily crack'd, and never well mended.

*

A long Life may not be good enough, but a good life is long enough.

Learning to the Studious; Riches to the Careful;
Power to the Bold; Heaven to the Virtuous.

*

The Brave and the Wise can both pity and excuse;
when Cowards and Fools shew no Mercy.

*

Good Sense and Learning may Esteem obtain
Humour and Wit a Laugh, if rightly ta'en;
· Fair Virtue Admiration may impart;
But 'tis GOOD-NATURE only wins the Heart:
It molds the Body to an easy Grace,
And brightens every Feature of the Face;
It smooths th' unpolish'd Tongue with Eloquence,
And adds Persuasion to the finest Sense.